A GOLDEN JUNIOR GUIDE

BEES, WASPS, and ANTS

A GOLDEN JUNIOR GUIDE™

BEES, WASPS, and ANTS

By GEORGE S. FICHTER
Illustrated by KRISTIN KEST

Consultant: Dr. Norman Platnick, Curator,
Department of Entomology, American Museum of Natural History

A GOLDEN BOOK • NEW YORK
Western Publishing Company, Inc., Racine, Wisconsin 53404

 Library of Congress Catalog Card Number: 92-73495 ISBN: 0-307-11434-1/ISBN: 0-307-61434-4 (lib. bdg.) A MCMXCIII

Bees, Wasps, and Ants are all insects. Like other insects, their bodies are divided into three parts: the head, thorax (middle), and abdomen (stomach). They have one pair of antennae and three pairs of legs. Most have two pairs of transparent wings. But many ants do not have any wings at all. A few have wings only at certain times in their lives. In this book, you'll meet some of the most commonly seen or familiar bees, wasps, and ants.

Did You Know?

Ants are social insects. Social insects live together in large groups called *colonies*. Some bees and wasps live in colonies, too. But most live alone.

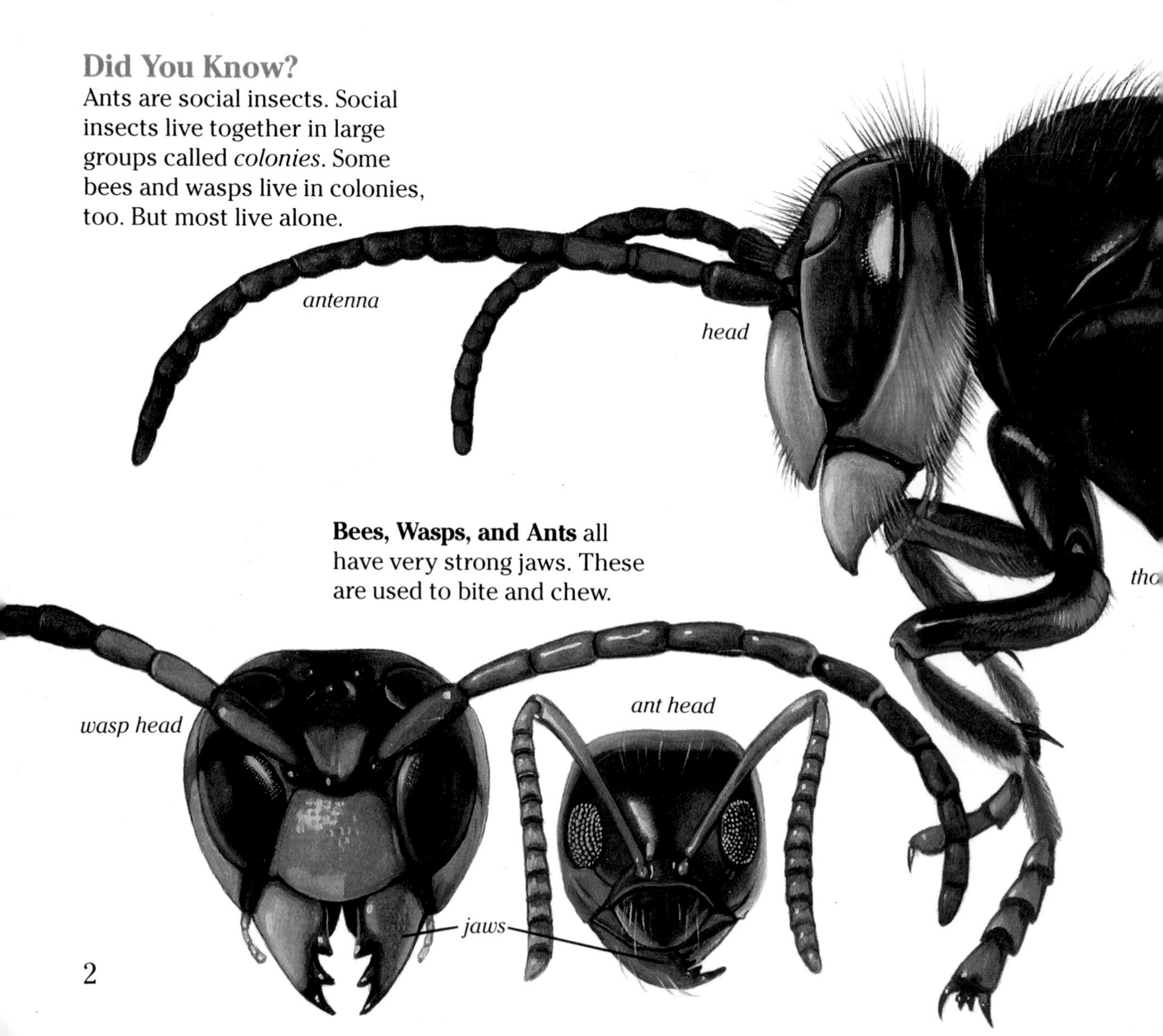

Bees, Wasps, and Ants all have very strong jaws. These are used to bite and chew.

:es and Wasps have
ɾge front wings. Smaller
ɪd wings are attached
the front wings with tiny,
ɔoklike structures. This
lows the wings to move
gether as one.

front wing

"hooks" on wings

hind wing

abdomen

stinger

ıd Hill Wasp

legs

Bees, Wasps, and Ants are the only insects with stingers.

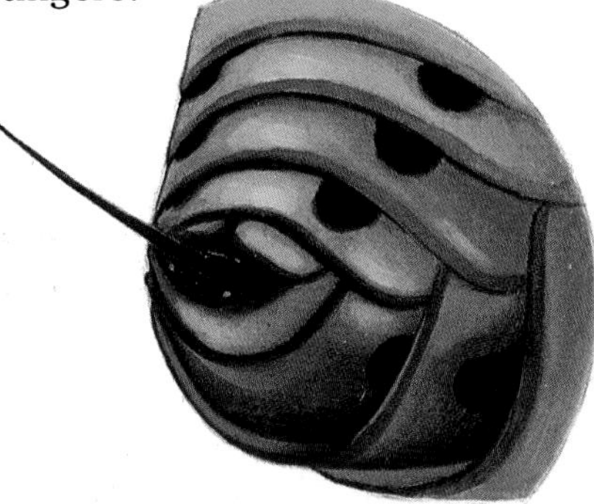

Did You Also Know?

There are more than 120,000 different kinds of bees, wasps, and ants.

How Can You Tell if an insect is a bee, a wasp, or an ant?

There are some clues you can look for.

Bees feed on *nectar*, the sweet fluid from flowers.

Bees

- ❑ Most bees have a heavy, rounded body.
- ❑ It is difficult to see the waist on a bee.
- ❑ Most bees have a very hairy body.

Wasps

- ❑ Wasps usually have a thin body.
- ❑ Most wasps have a thin, threadlike waist.
- ❑ Most wasps have little or no hair on their body.

Ants

- ❑ Most ants do not have wings.
- ❑ An ant has a slim waist with one or two "bumps" near the middle.
- ❑ The antennae of ants are bent where the longer parts join the shorter parts. This forms a kind of "elbow."

Wasps eat mainly spiders, insects, and other small animals.

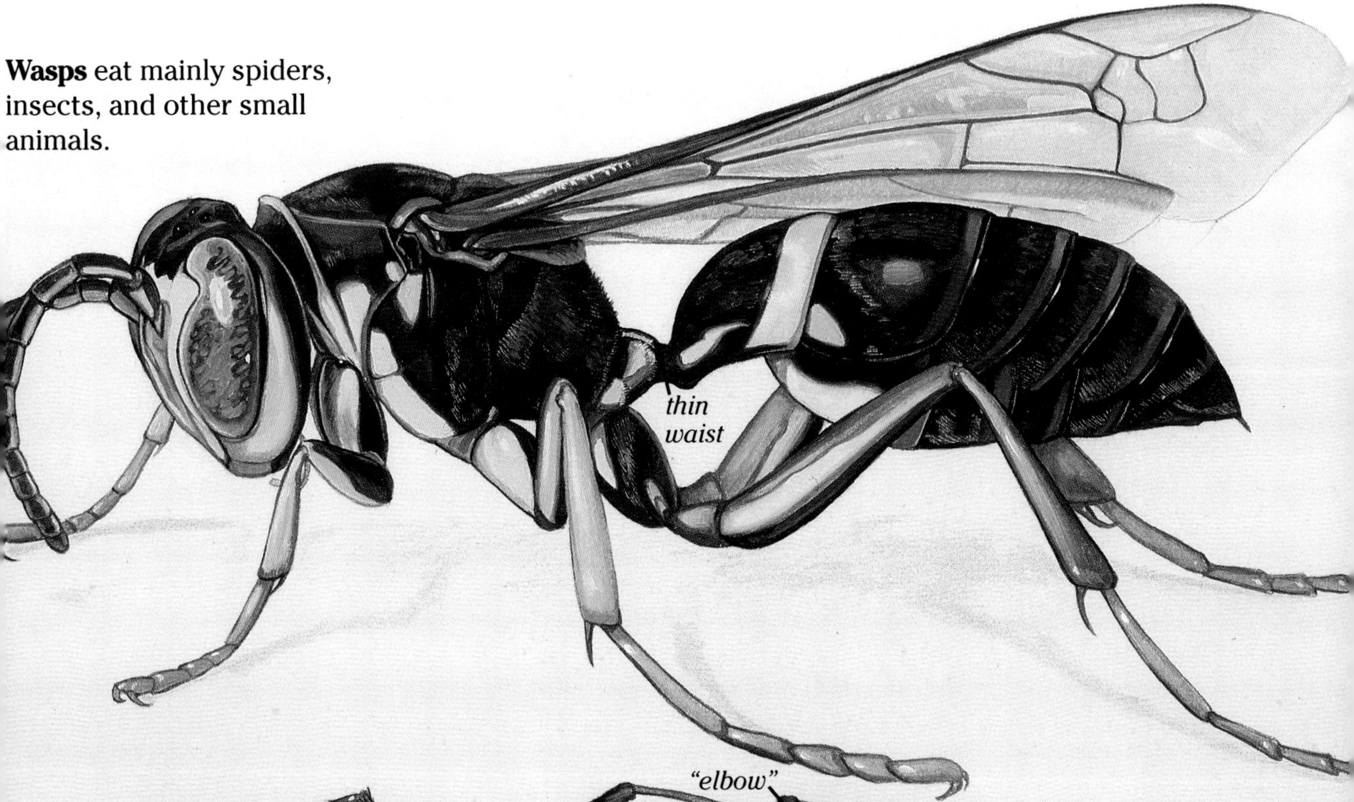

thin waist

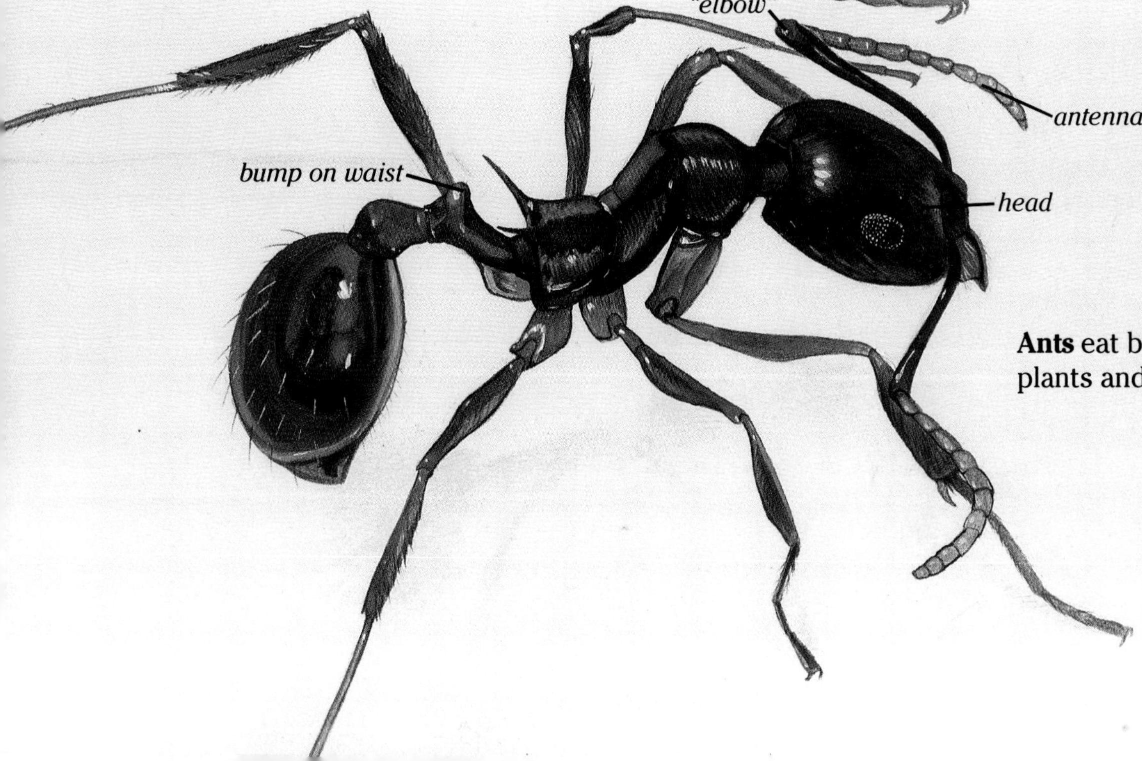

"elbow"

antenna

bump on waist

head

Ants eat both plants and animals.

A Colony of bees, wasps, or ants may contain thousands of individuals! All the members of the colony have special jobs to do. A small colony usually has one queen, some males, and many workers—all females. The queen is a large female. It is her job to lay all the eggs for the colony. Bees mate while flying. Several males may successfully mate with the queen in a single "mating flight." This means that the babies that are later produced may have more than one father.

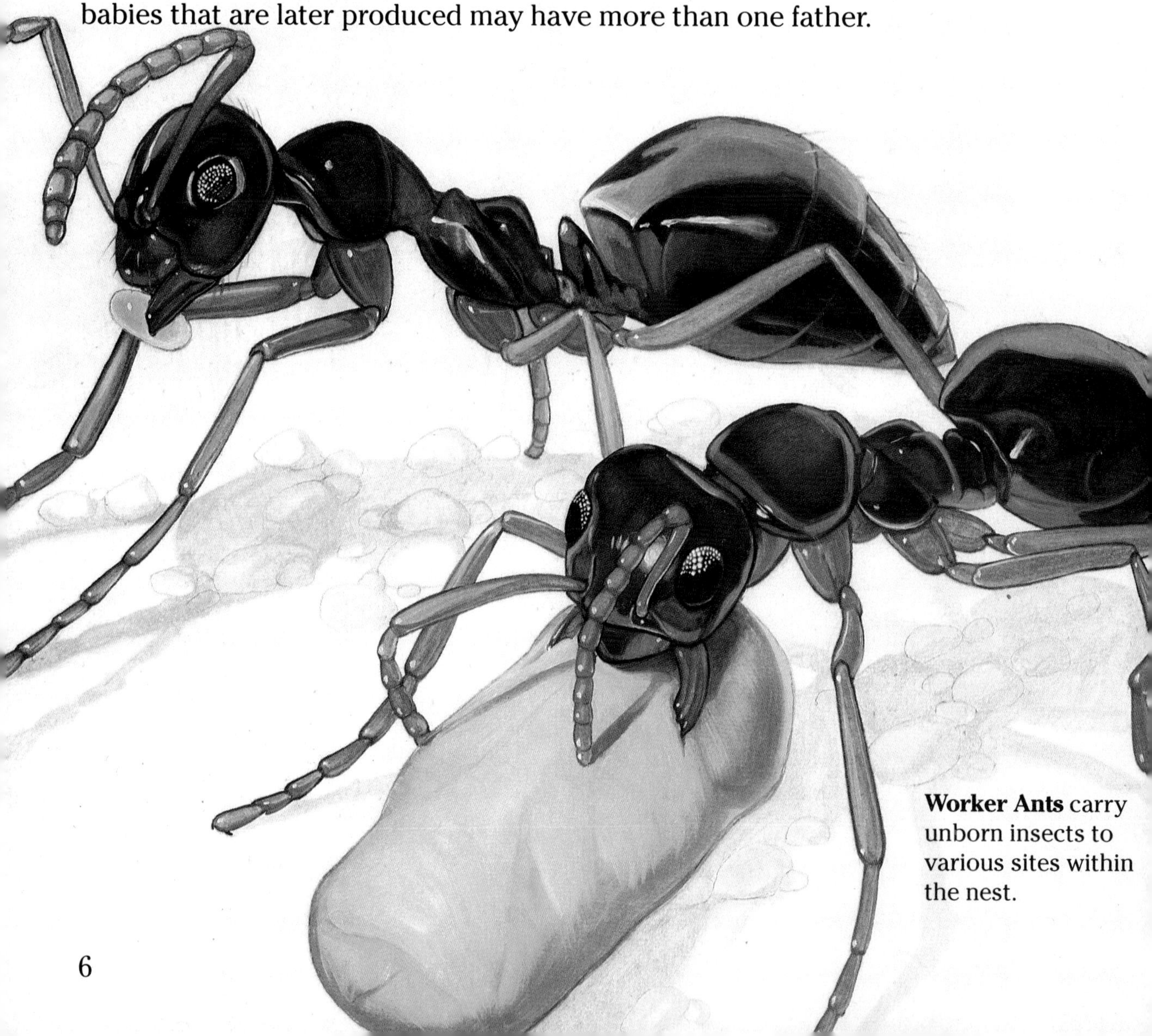

Worker Ants carry unborn insects to various sites within the nest.

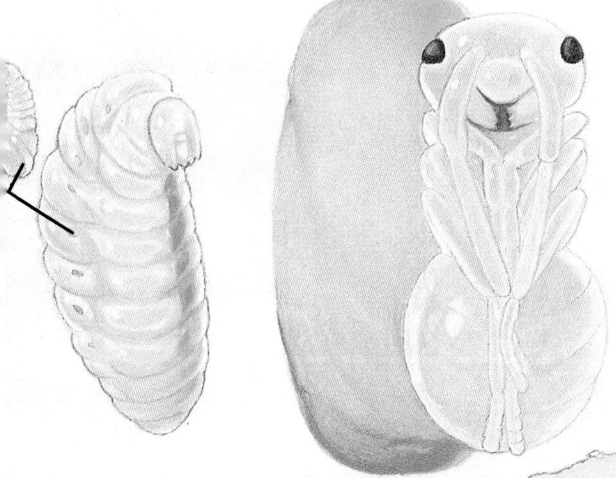

pupa and pupal case

Did You Know?

Every bee, wasp, and ant goes through four stages in life. First, it is an egg. When the egg hatches, the baby–called a *larva*–begins feeding on food an adult has brought to the nest. After a few weeks, the larva changes into what is called a *pupa*. By the end of the pupal stage, the insect has taken on the shape of an adult!

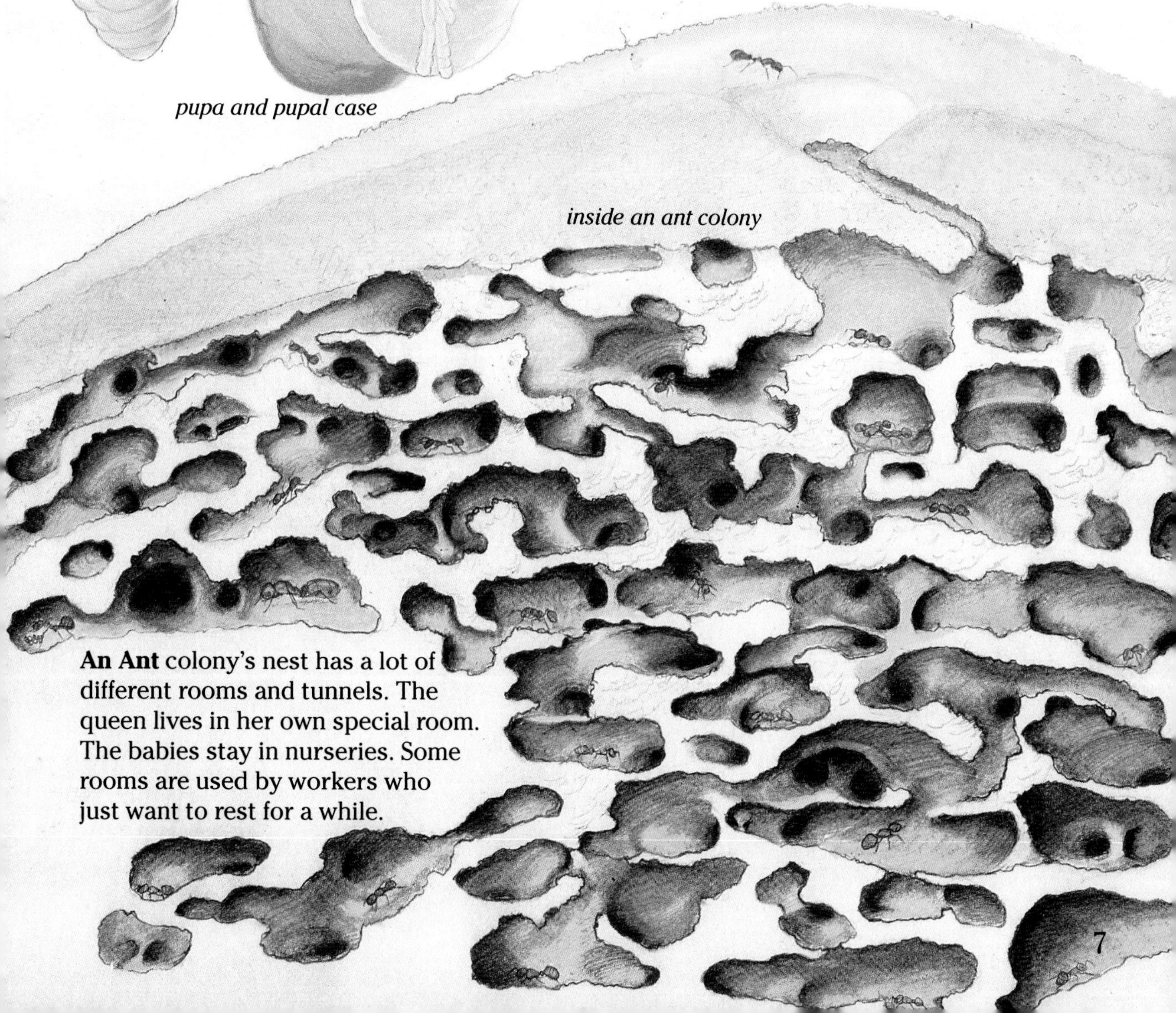

inside an ant colony

An Ant colony's nest has a lot of different rooms and tunnels. The queen lives in her own special room. The babies stay in nurseries. Some rooms are used by workers who just want to rest for a while.

Honeybees make honey from nectar and pollen. Pollen, a yellow "dust," is an important food for bee larvae. As a bee travels from flower to flower, grains of pollen stick to the hairs on its body. Some of the pollen rubs off when the bee visits another flower. The flower uses the newly acquired pollen to make seeds from which new plants will grow.

pollen basket

pollen in pollen basket

Honeybees have little pollen "baskets" on their hind legs. These are made up of many short, stiff hairs. The bees use the pollen baskets to carry pollen back to the colony.

A Honeybee will sting to protect itself or its colony. Its stinger has tiny hooks, or barbs, on it. These hooks prevent the stinger from being withdrawn. The stinger, with its poison sac, usually pulls out of the bee's body, staying in the wound. After losing its stinger, a Honeybee dies.

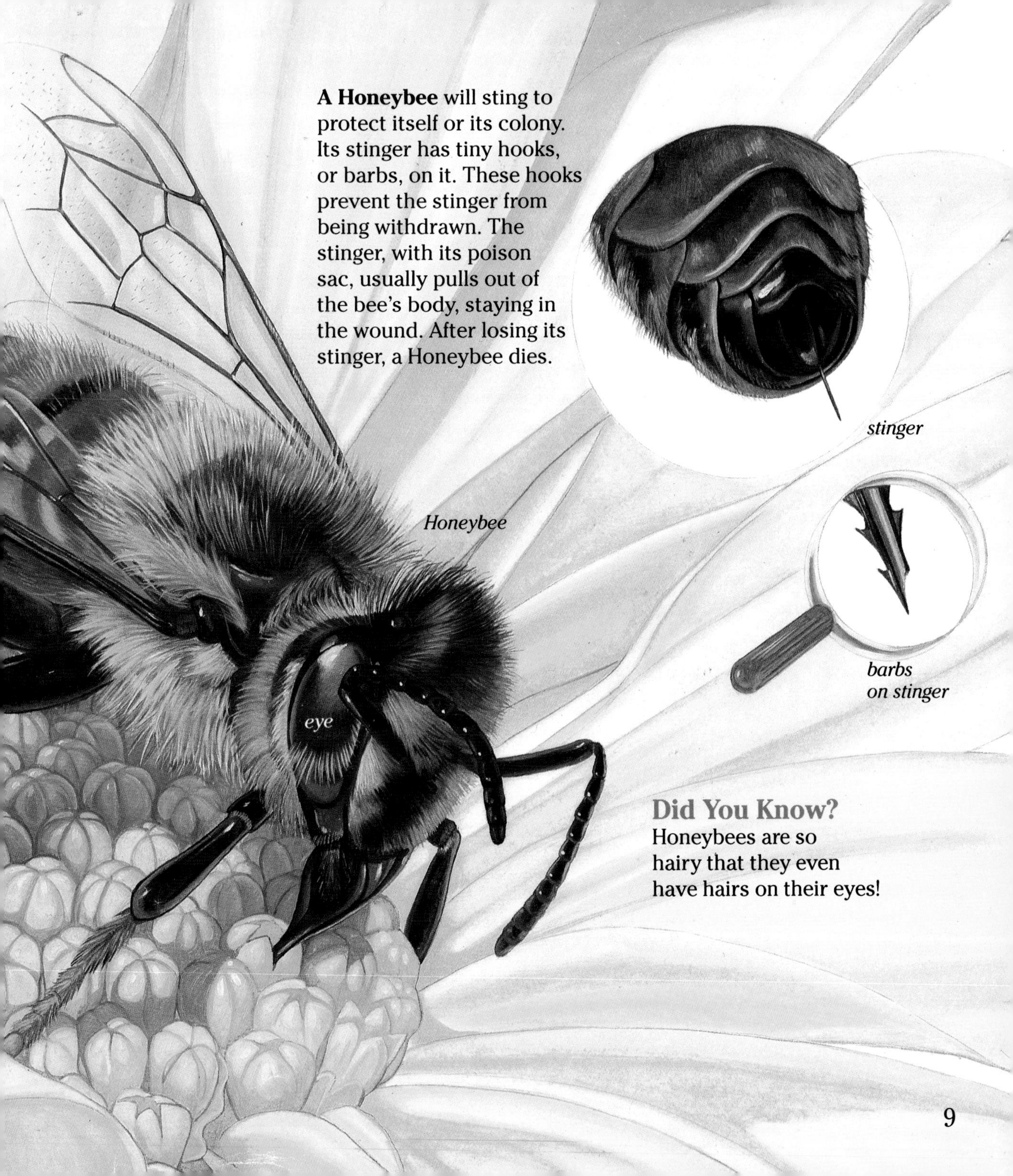

stinger

Honeybee

barbs on stinger

eye

Did You Know?

Honeybees are so hairy that they even have hairs on their eyes!

To Build a Home for the Honeybee colony, workers make wax and shape it into *honeycombs.* The wax is made in the bee's abdomen. The hundreds of six-sided little "rooms" of the honeycomb are called its *cells.* Some cells are used by the queen for her eggs. Other cells are used to store pollen and nectar. The cells of the honeycomb are also used to make honey. The bees eat the honey mostly in the winter months, when it is too cold to go outside. The cells of the honeycomb have very thin walls, but they are strong enough to hold a lot of honey.

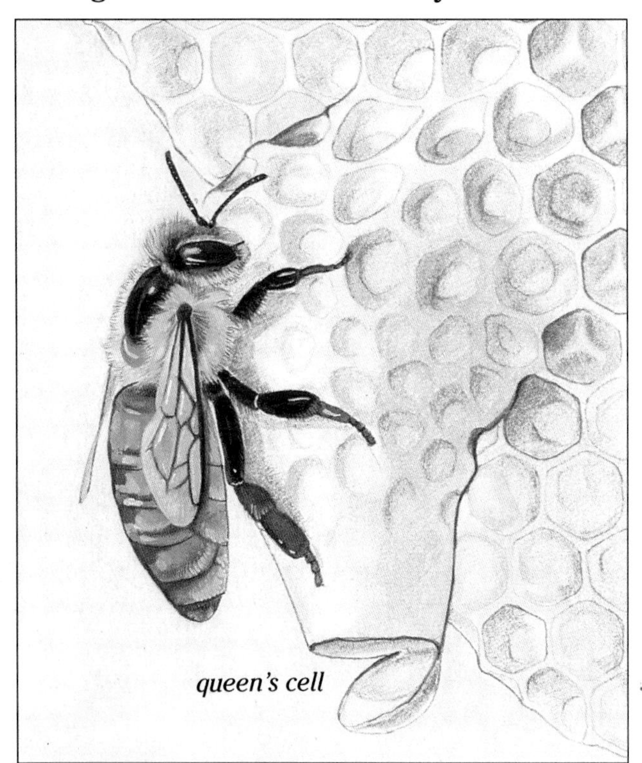

Honeybee queens have special cells built for them. The queen's cell is about the size of a peanut shell. It is the largest cell in the honeycomb.

empty cell

pollen stored in cell

Did You Know?

A Honeybee queen may lay more than 2,000 eggs every day!

Honeybee workers live for only about two months, during the busy summer season. A queen Honeybee may live for three years.

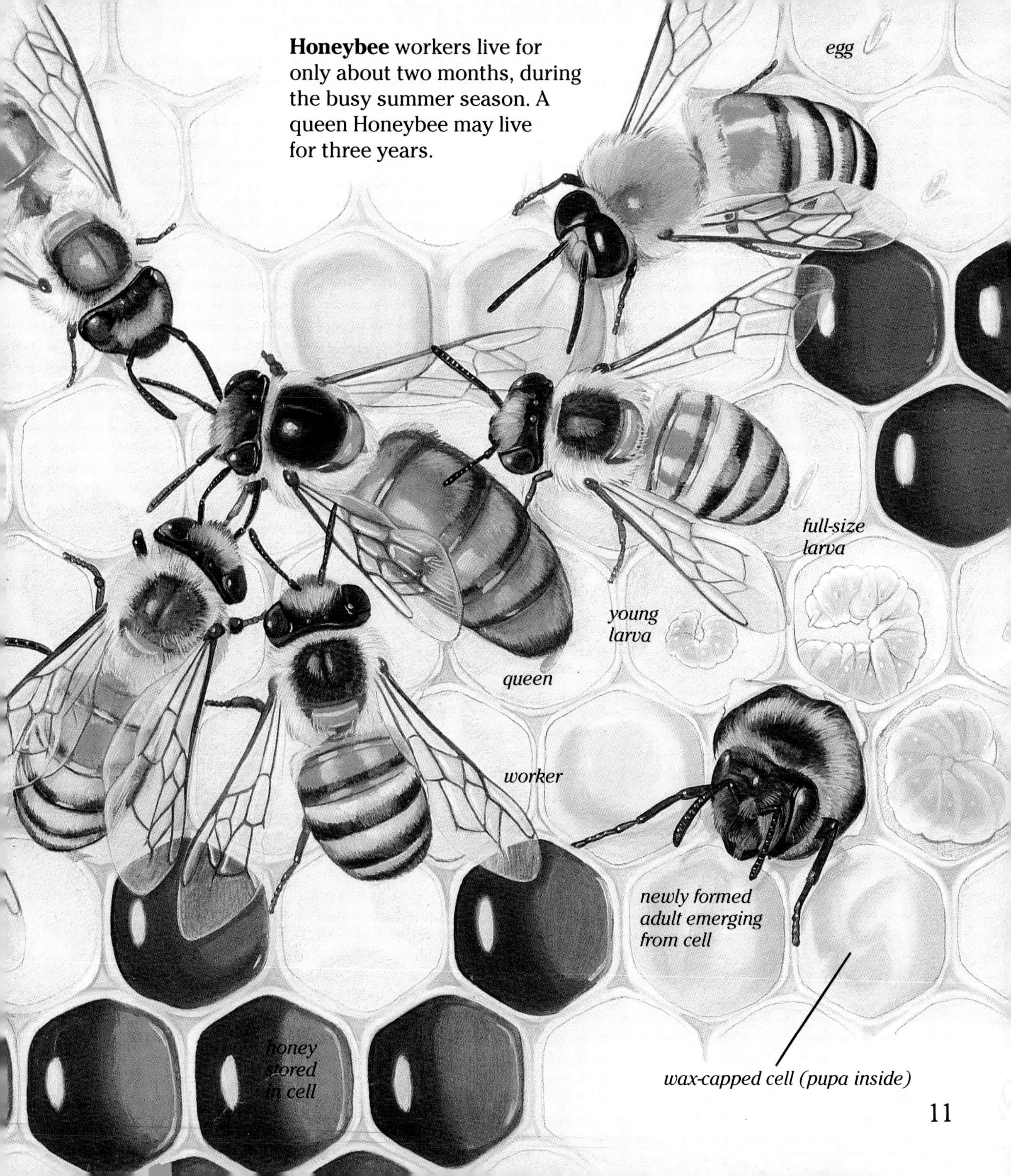

egg

full-size larva

young larva

queen

worker

newly formed adult emerging from cell

honey stored in cell

wax-capped cell (pupa inside)

The Life of a Honeybee Colony is very busy. Thousands of workers scurry about doing their various jobs. Nurse workers care for the babies. Housekeepers clean waste materials and dead bees from cells. Some workers stand guard to protect the nest from enemies. Other workers fly off in search of food to bring back to the colony. A lot is always going on—inside and outside the nest!

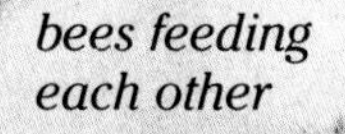

Did You Know?
Worker bees usually work very hard. But sometimes a bee will take a vacation and do no work at all for a few days!

If a Honeybee colony becomes too crowded, the queen and many of the workers will fly off together to build a new nest. This is called *swarming*.

Did You Also Know?

A swarm of Honeybees may contain thousands of insects!

Worker Bees do special "dances" at the nest. In one dance, they tell other bees about nectar they have found. They describe where it is and whether they have found a little or a lot.

Bumblebees are large bees, usually yellow and black in color. Some Bumblebees are twice as large as Honeybees. A Bumblebee also has an extra-long tongue for sipping the nectar from deep inside flowers such as red clover. Few other bees have such long tongues. Like Honeybees, Bumblebees have pollen baskets on their hind legs. Clumps of pollen stick to the Bumblebee's legs as it sips the nectar. Some of this pollen is rubbed off as the bee travels from flower to flower. This helps new plants to spread.

Did You Know?

A Bumblebee's stinger is smooth and slides right out of a wound. Because of this, the Bumblebee does not die after it stings and may sting again and again!

Bumblebee

Bumblebees don't build honeycombs. They live in nests. Wax produced by the queen may be shaped into "honeypots" that are placed in the nest. These store nectar as well as a honeylike mixture of pollen and nectar.

Did You Also Know?

Bumblebees make their nests in damp ground, rotting logs, or buildings. Sometimes they will move into an empty mouse nest!

honeypot

Bumblebee nest

red clover flower

Did You Also Know?

A Bumblebee queen usually survives the winter in the nest. But the worker bees die. In spring, the queen lays her eggs in the nest, and the colony comes back to life.

Leaf-cutter Bees make their nests in hollow plant stems or in tunnels bored in wood. The female cuts small circles from leaves or flower petals. She creates a little room, or cell, with them. Then she mixes together pollen and nectar. She puts the mixture in the cell, lays an egg on top, and seals the entrance with more bits of leaves. When the egg hatches, the larva has lots of food to eat. It stays in the cell until it is almost an adult. Leaf-cutter Bees do not live together in large groups.

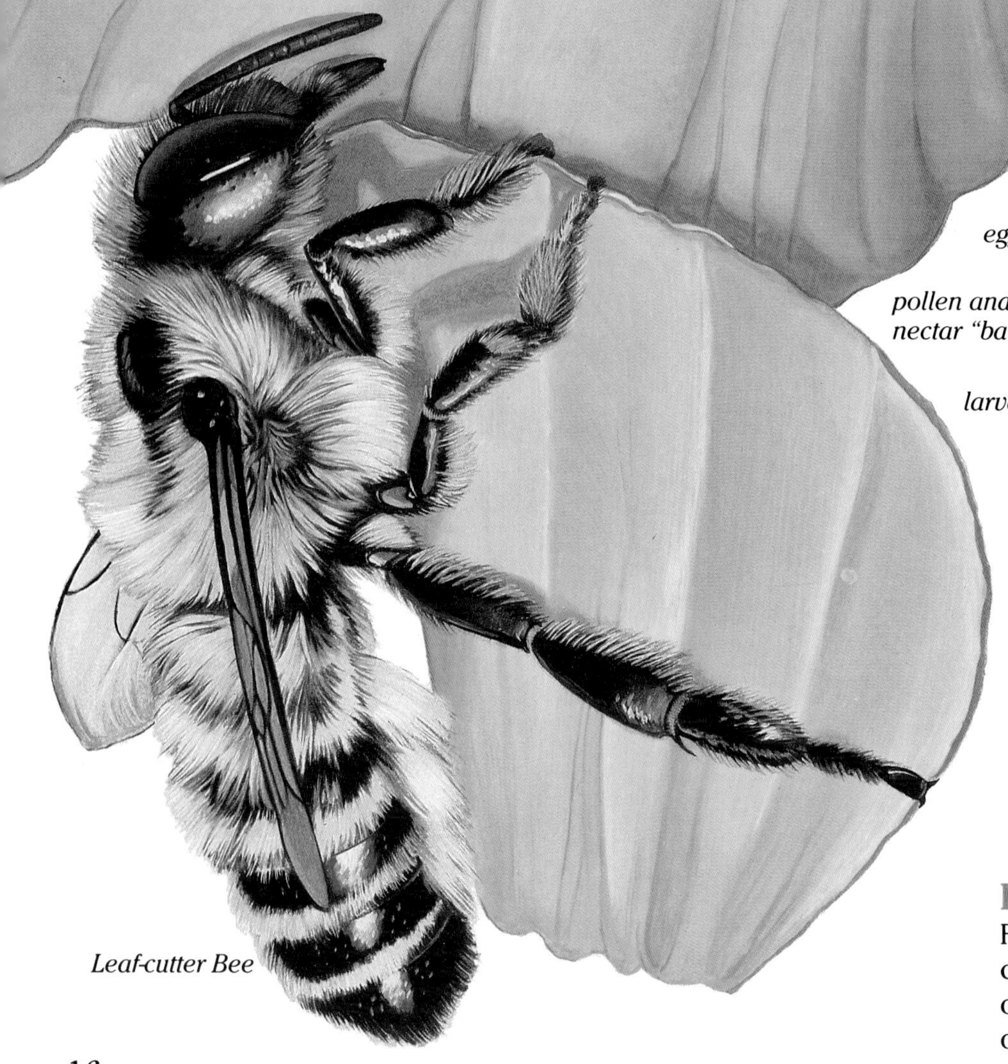

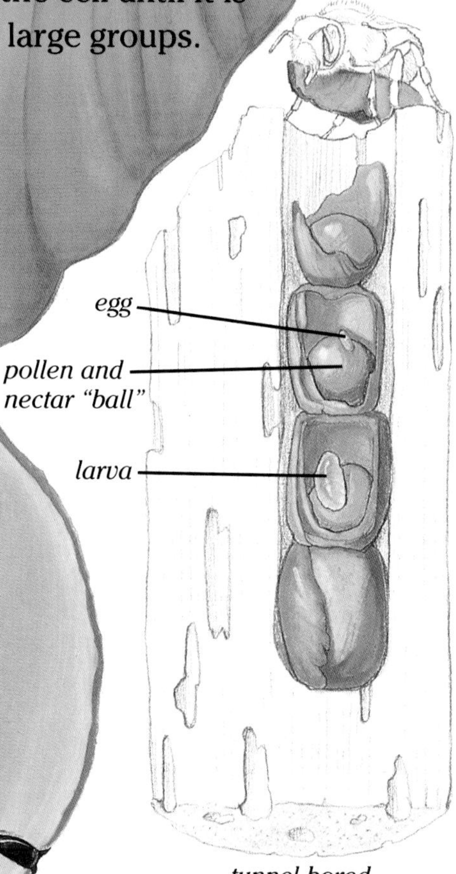

tunnel bored in wood

Leaf-cutter Bee

Did You Know?

Female Leaf-cutter Bees carry their pollen loads on their abdomen, not on their legs.

Carpenter Bees make their nests by chewing holes in wood. Although these bees may build their nests near each other, they do not live together as a colony. One kind of Carpenter Bee is quite big. It looks a lot like a Bumblebee. But many are small and are shiny blue, green, or black in color.

Carpenter Bee

Did You Know?

Like other insects, bees do not have lungs. They breathe through tiny holes, called *spiracles*, on the sides of their bodies.

Mud Daubers are various wasps that make nests out of mud. These nests may be found under roofs or attached to ceilings or other places where they will not get wet. Mud Daubers live alone. They also hunt for food alone. Like a bee's nest, a Mud Dauber's home is made up of many cells. These are used mostly for storing eggs.

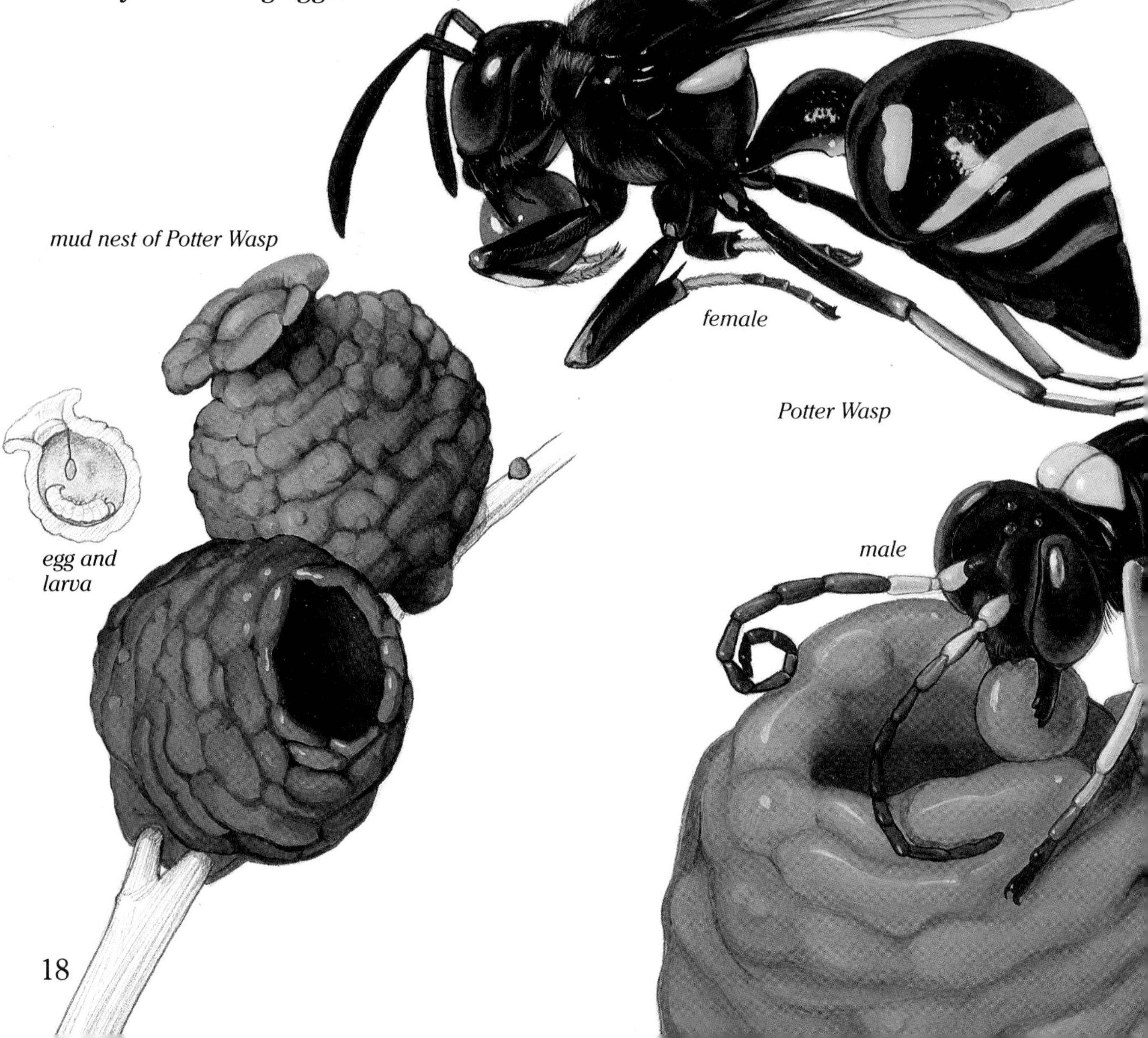

mud nest of Potter Wasp

female

Potter Wasp

egg and larva

male

The Female Mud Dauber stings spiders. But instead of killing them with her sting, she paralyzes them. She then puts one or two in each cell in her nest. She lays an egg and seals the cell shut. When the larvae hatch from the eggs, they will have a good supply of fresh food to eat!

egg and paralyzed spider inside nest

Common Mud Dauber building its nest

Paper Wasps were given this name because they really do make paper! They chew up wood or other plant matter. Then they mix it with saliva to make the paper. They use the paper to build their nest. The nest hangs from a sturdy stem under a roof or in some other protected place.

Paper Wasp

A Paper Wasp will sting again and again to protect itself or its colony!

Did You Know?

Many years ago, a Frenchman noticed how wasps made paper from wood. He copied the wasps and made the first modern paper. We still make paper almost the same way today.

silk-covered cell, pupa inside

egg

larva

Paper Wasp nest

Yellow Jackets and Hornets are close relatives of Paper Wasps. Yellow Jackets often make their nests under logs or rocks. Hornet nests are bigger. Thousands of Hornets may live in just one huge nest. Made of paper, the nest is hung from the branches of a tree or bush. Its entrance is at the bottom.

Yellow Jackets are black with wide yellow bands. Most Hornets are black with yellowish-white spots.

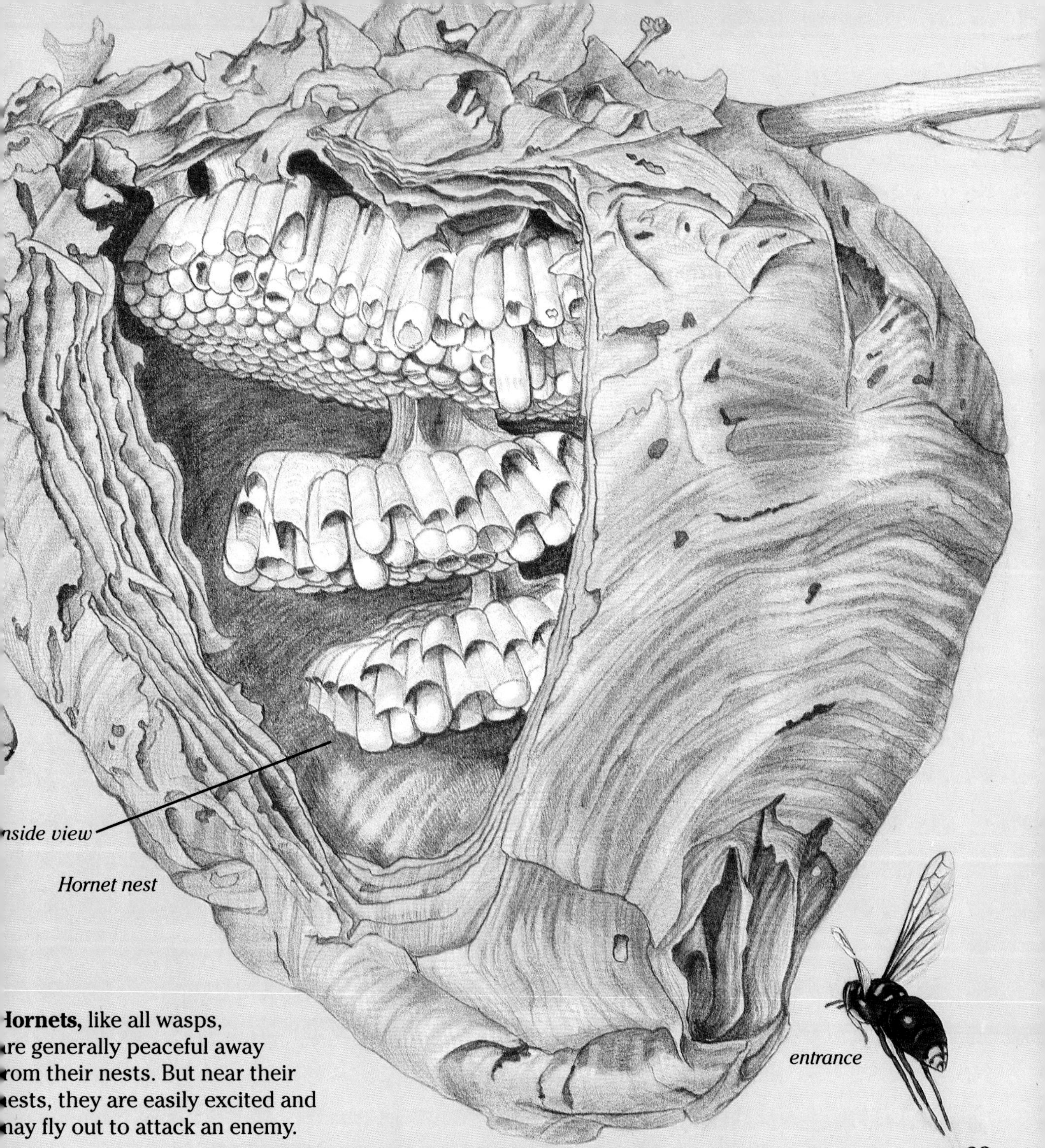

nside view

Hornet nest

entrance

Iornets, like all wasps,
re generally peaceful away
rom their nests. But near their
ests, they are easily excited and
nay fly out to attack an enemy.

Cicada Killers are very large wasps. They may grow to be more than 1½ inches long. Cicada Killers do not live in colonies, and they hunt alone. They dig long burrows and lay their eggs in them. Cicada Killers attack cicadas. These are large insects that buzz noisily in trees and bushes. The cicadas are used as food for wasp larvae.

1. The Female Cicada Killer paralyzes the cicada with a sting, then carries it back to her burrow.

2. Inside the Nest, the female Cicada Killer lays an egg on top of the cicada. Then she seals the entrance to the burrow.

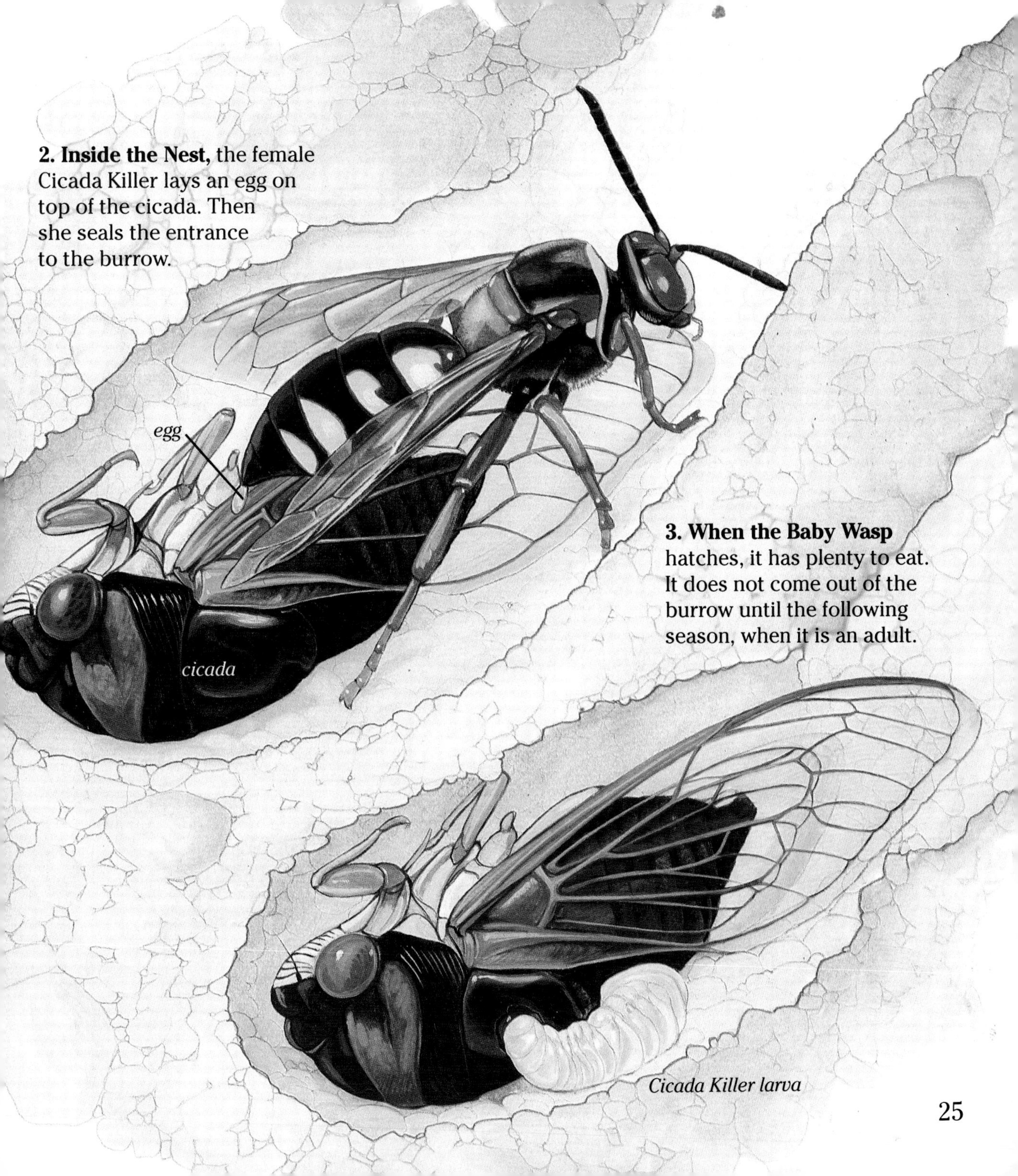

egg

cicada

3. When the Baby Wasp hatches, it has plenty to eat. It does not come out of the burrow until the following season, when it is an adult.

Cicada Killer larva

Velvet Ants are not ants at all. They are wasps! They are called ants because the females, which have no wings, look like ants. Most kinds of Velvet Ants have a thick, velvety coat, with bright red and black bands. Velvet Ants are also called Cow Killers because of their powerful sting.

Velvet Ants move rapidly along the ground as they hunt for prey.

Velvet Ants

stinger

Did You Know?

Velvet Ants usually search for food in dry, sandy areas. When they find the burrow of a wasp or bee, they sting the insect to kill it. Then they lay their eggs on whatever food the other insect had in its burrow!

Did You Also Know?

Female Velvet Ants do not have wings. But they do have stingers. Male Velvet Ants have wings—but no stingers.

male

female

Cornfield Ants are the brownish red ants commonly seen in yards or gardens. They like to make their nests along the sides of and beneath sidewalks. Sometimes they nest inside houses. But most of the time they stay outdoors. They like to eat the sweet drops of honeydew given off by green plant lice called *aphids*. They "milk" the aphids by stroking them with their antennae. This makes the honeydew flow. Sometimes the ants herd these little insects like cattle, bringing them to plants where the aphids can feed. They will also take them into their nests to protect them in bad weather.

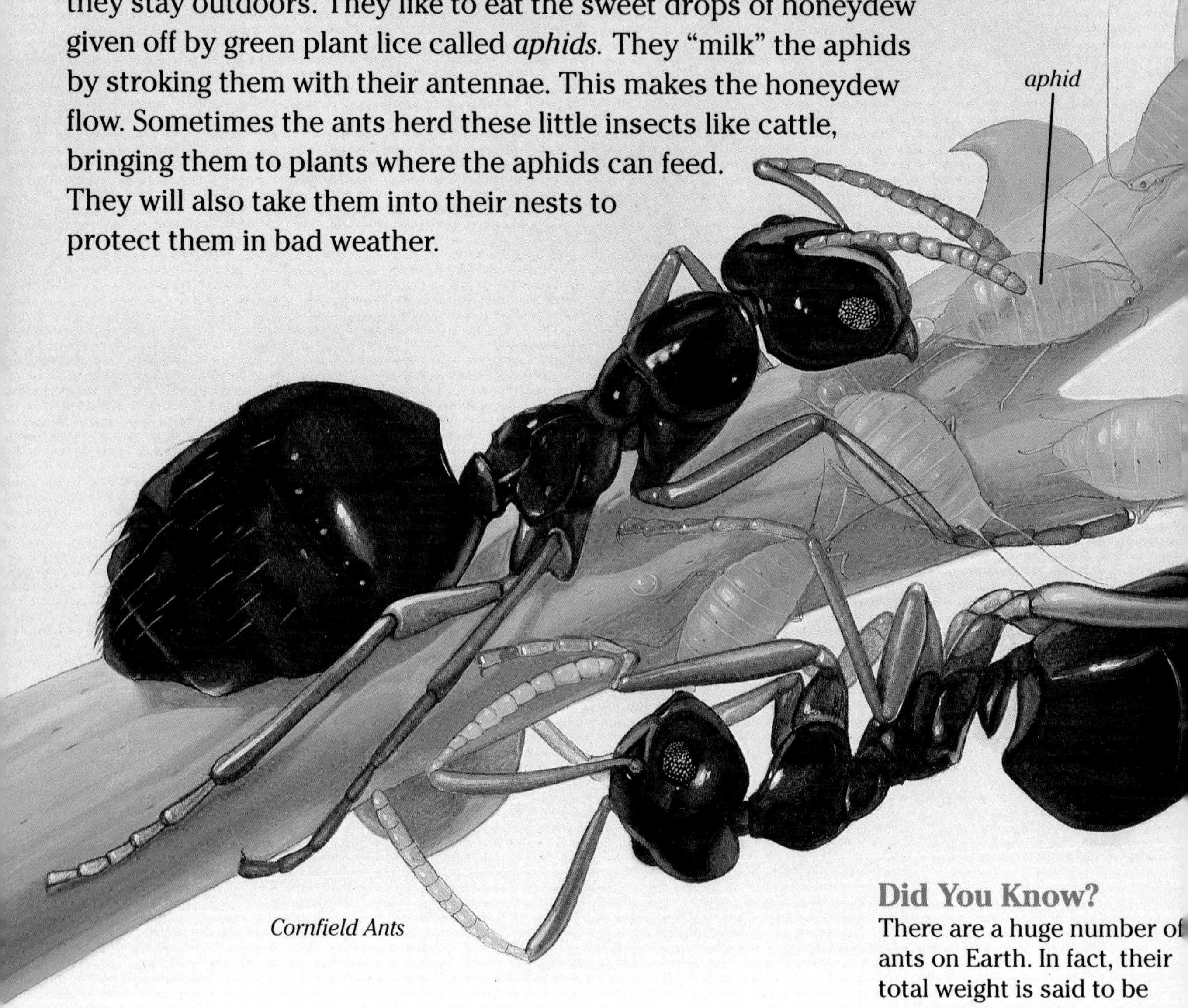

aphid

Cornfield Ants

Did You Know?

There are a huge number of ants on Earth. In fact, their total weight is said to be greater than that of all other land animals combined!

Did You Also Know?

Ants can float, but they cannot swim. To cross puddles of water, they form a chain with their own bodies. To cross a flowing stream, a group of ants form their bodies into a moving, rolling ball.

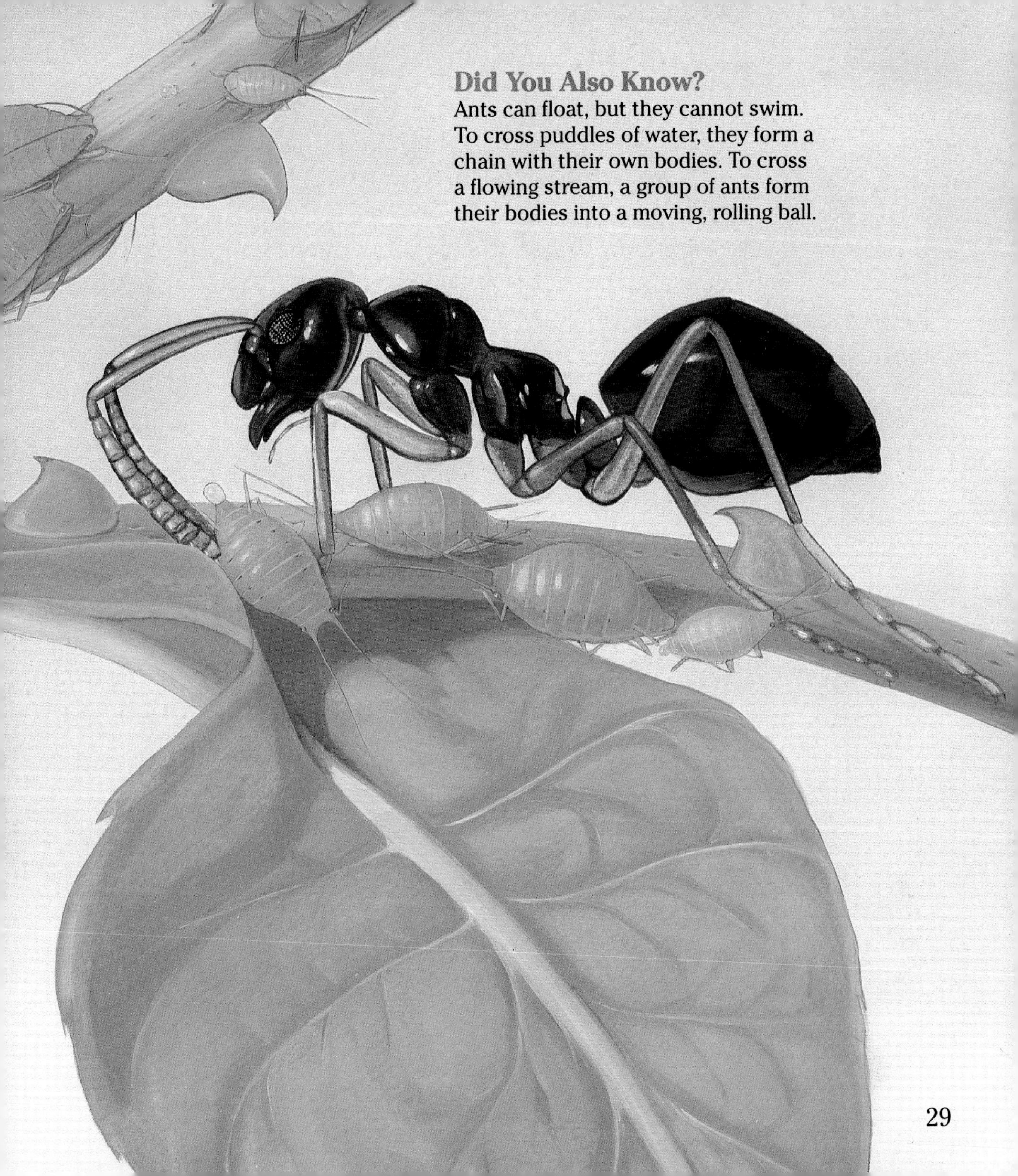

Carpenter Ants make their nests in wood. They do not eat the wood, as termites do, but in cutting passageways through it, they can do a lot of damage! They usually cut into rotting logs, but sometimes they will attack wooden buildings or other wooden structures. Carpenter Ants may be up to half an inch long. With their powerful jaws, they can give a painful bite.

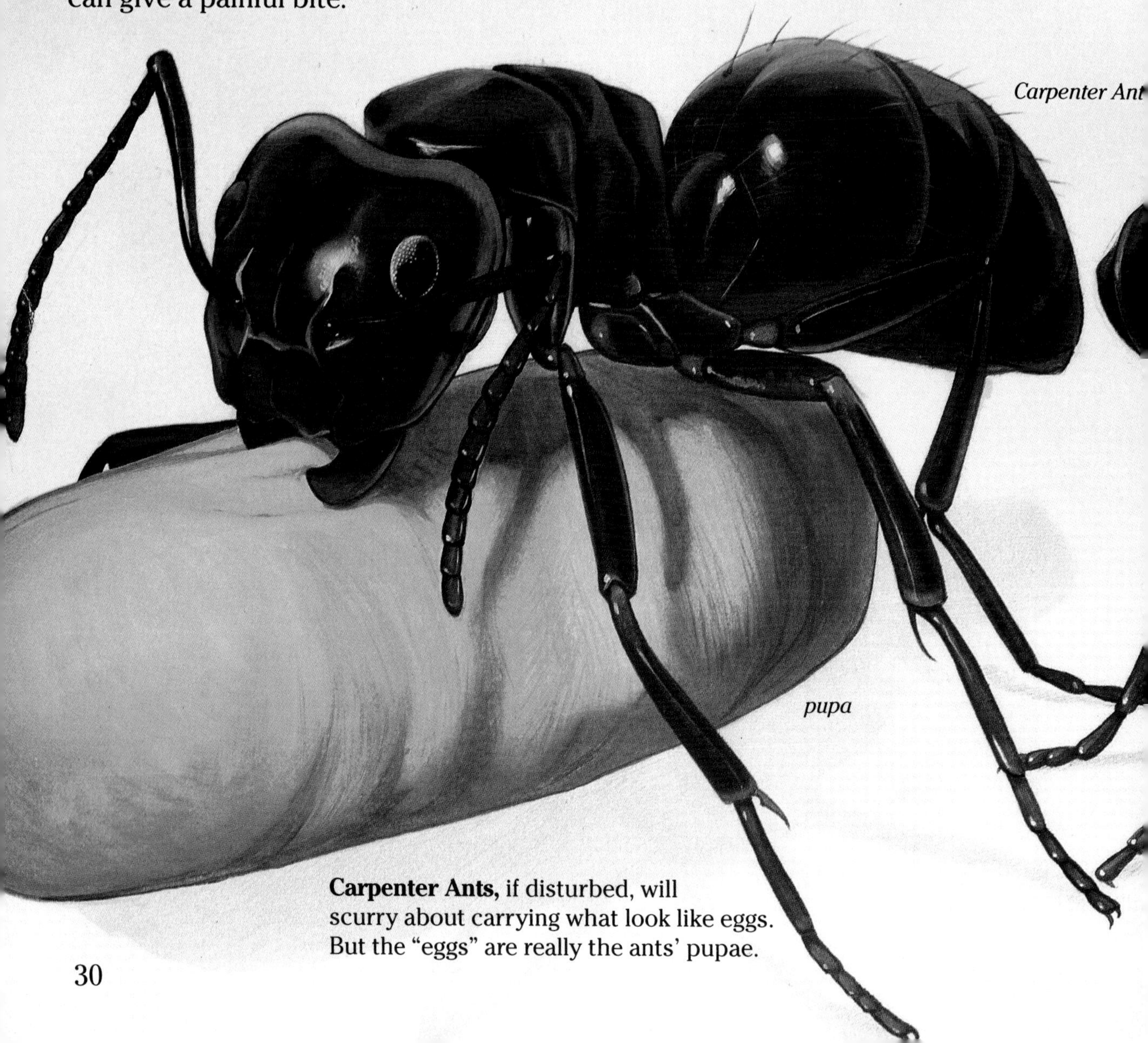

Carpenter Ant

pupa

Carpenter Ants, if disturbed, will scurry about carrying what look like eggs. But the "eggs" are really the ants' pupae.

Did You Know?

A queen ant can live for more than 15 years! Worker ants live for about a year.

Did You Also Know?

Ants use their antennae to taste, smell, touch, and hear!

Crazy Ants and Pharaoh Ants are common household pests. Crazy Ants have long legs. They seem to run around without knowing where they are going. Then suddenly they disappear! The smaller Pharaoh Ant makes itself at home in many different and unlikely places. Sometimes the Pharaoh Ant is called the Sugar Ant. This is because it likes to eat cookie crumbs and other sugary tidbits. But candies and cooking oils are its favorite foods.

Crazy Ant

Both Crazy Ants and Pharaoh Ants prefer to live outdoors in summer or in warm climates. But as soon as the weather turns cool, they move inside.

Pharaoh Ants can be found anywhere in the house, from the basement to an upstairs bedroom. They live in the countryside and in big cities. These pesky ants are harmless, though. They annoy people simply because they "get into" things.

Pharaoh Ants

Fire Ants live in pastures and yards and along grassy roadways. They feed on seeds, fruits, and even small animals. Fire Ants give painful stings that feel like sharp, burning stabs. An attack by many of them at once can hurt a lot. Most amazingly, the first Fire Ant to sting releases a chemical that tells all the other ants to sting, too!

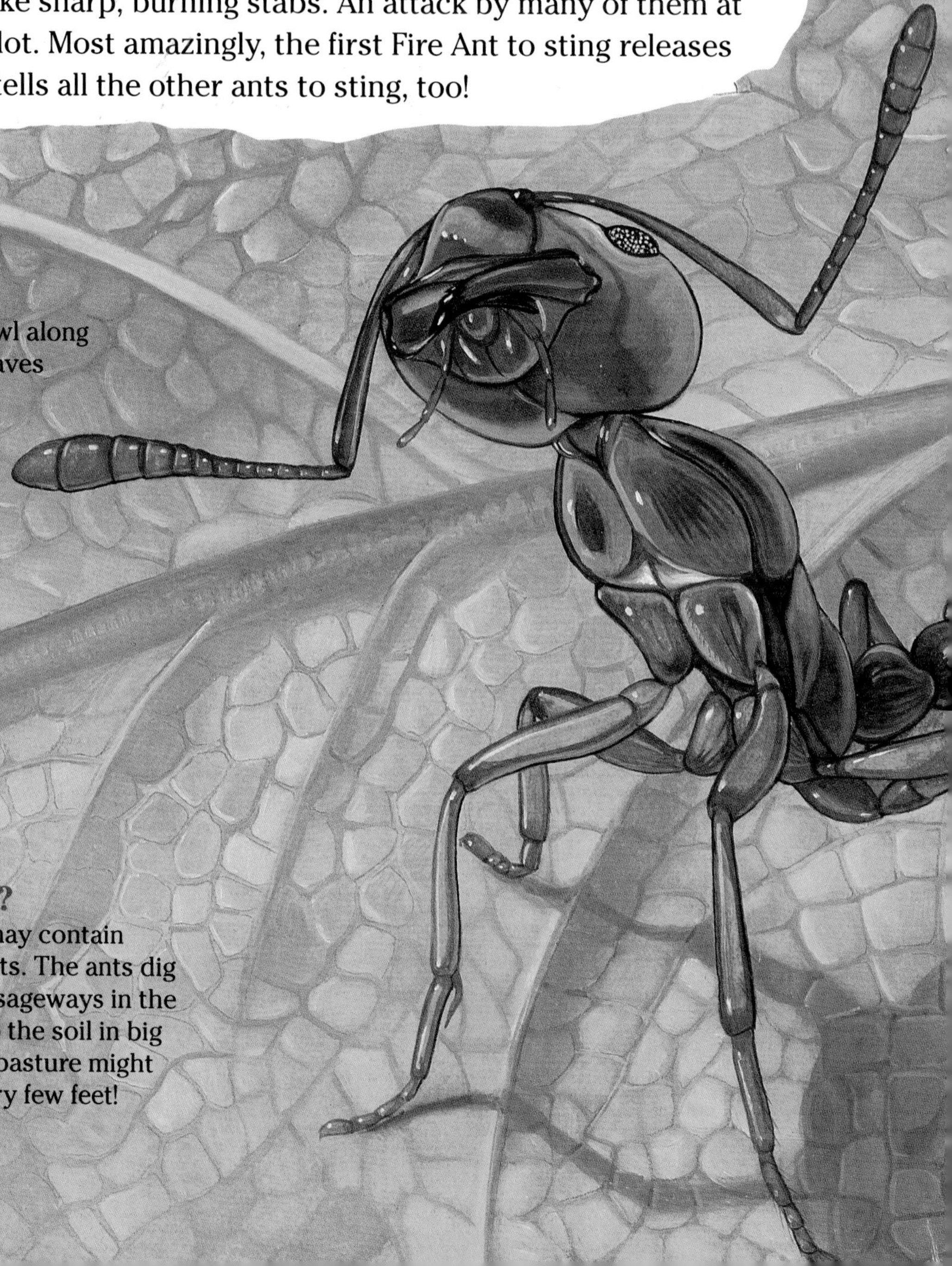

Fire Ants often crawl along the underside of leaves looking for food.

Did You Know?

Fire Ant colonies may contain thousands of insects. The ants dig chambers and passageways in the earth. They pile up the soil in big mounds. A grassy pasture might have a mound every few feet!

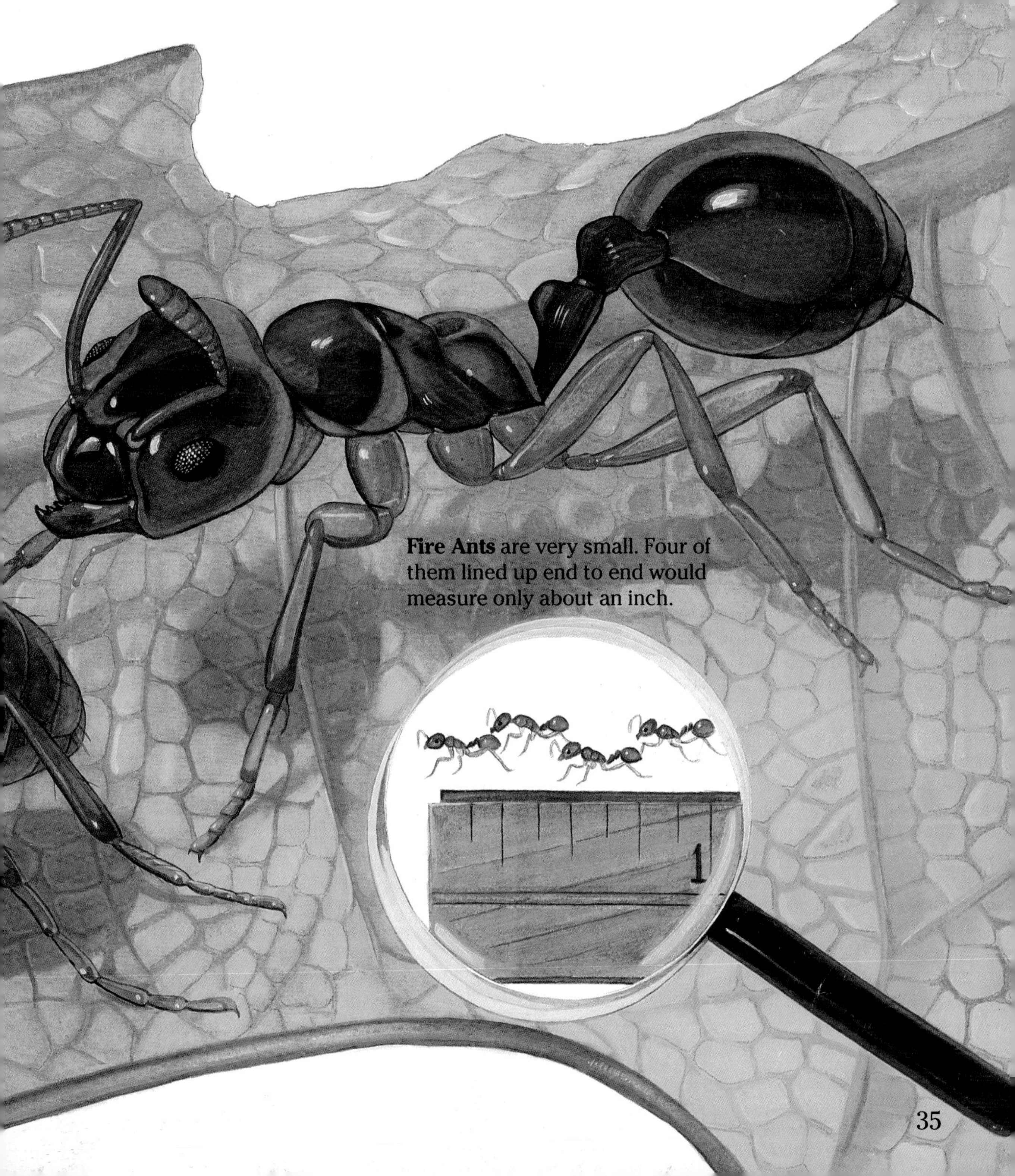

Fire Ants are very small. Four of them lined up end to end would measure only about an inch.

For Further Reading

With this book, you've only just begun to explore some exciting new worlds. Why not continue to learn about the wonderful creatures known as bees, wasps, and ants? For example, you might want to browse through *Insects (a Golden Guide),* which contains many fascinating details on the species in this book and others as well. Another Golden Book you might enjoy is *The Golden Book of Insects and Spiders.* Also, be sure to visit your local library, where you will discover a variety of titles on the subject.

Index